NECK OF THE WOODS

By the Same Author

POETRY

Ato (Pine Wave Press, 2002)

CRITICISM

Provence and Pound (University of California Press, 1979)
Pound's Cantos (Johns Hopkins University Press, 1992)
Bunting: The Shaping of His Verse (Clarendon Press, 1997)

AS EDITOR

Basil Bunting on Poetry (Johns Hopkins University Press, 1999)
Ezra Pound's Cantos: A Casebook (Oxford University Press, 2006)

NECK *of the* WOODS

PETER MAKIN

ISOBAR
PRESS

Published in 2015 by

Isobar Press
Sakura 2-21-23-202, Setagaya-ku,
Tokyo 156-0053, Japan
&
14 Isokon Flats, Lawn Road,
London NW3 2XD, United Kingdom

http://isobarpress.com

ISBN 978-4-907359-12-6

ACKNOWLEDGEMENTS

An earlier version of 'Ato' was published as a book by Pine
Wave Press (2002); 'Hagoromo' (also in an earlier version),
'Life-sketch' and 'Neck of the Woods' were first published
in *Shearsman*, and 'Percepticules' in *Damn the Caesars*.

Calligraphy on page 68 by the late Seika Kawabe; cover
photograph and photograph on page 55 by Peter Makin.

Contents

Life-sketch

I

Lincolnshire

Clean clearwater sand
out beyond the rubble and shore-wrack

a thin stream
cutting its own bed as you diverted it
tiny sharp grains
on inside bends,
forking across plains

half a centimetre
in unmarked sand.

I asked my fader what the well was
that made a deep hollow gurgling in the sand
he picked me up and
under the thick mossy planks
an infinity of water
rushing under the beach to the sea.

II

Lincolnshire

Pregnate
a hollow in the sands where the wispy
harsh grass

dusk gathered
a grey silent
depth over everything.

Sweaty summer night,
light taking years to fade

parents
out

III

Mali

A hedge, all round,
with great trees. Ridges,
with the earth muddied from the watering and then dried,
splashes like clay,
with the green plants pushing out of it.
I could have been happy there.
The hedge, and outside, the great plain.

Across the rice-plain the raised road.

Looking down through the trees by the road,
the turn of the furrow, the man on the tractor
to far out on the plain, turns
and returns unendingly.

IV

Lincolnshire

Amber mound,
frizz black, light
limbs displayed.

Bang the gong of
her delight.

In the green dawn
the thick tome in many tongues,
the pigeons,
the power.

V

Hiroshima

Silence, the
odour of clean sanitary arrangements,
the train-cries.

Pissing the piss of loneliness, the old
ripe brewery-smell through the window.

Silent student of the ways of men
in bars, gazing at smoke-furred plyboard;
listening.

A weaseled little office-worker, ill-shaven, grey,
feet planted apart
mouth set in a sort of twisted irony,

fatigue his alibi.

VI

Osaka

And so he tried to please them who despised each other,
his smiling white faces hither and thither
wet bat-wings against this rock, that wall

*

The sedge bowed down towards the sun
with the snow on it,
the sun melting it off
and breaking down the cells
slowly.

*

The mountainside fierce with cherryblossoms
and the ground already flecked with them

the day already
rife with excuses.

VII

Osaka / Lincolnshire

The rains have come and the river is full, and the souls of all the
little dead fishes carried down to dissolve in the great sea.

Dredging in the well
the wet fibres of leaf
droop over the fingers,
black fluid
descending to
black fluid.

Old glitter of darkness;
empty;
gaze.

Bang her gong.
He'll find the courage of his caution,
I wouldn't be in her shoes. Twenty years!

I wouldn't be in her shoes.

VIII

North Kyoto

Dim *&* green, with the damp air emanating

only the two troglodytes working at the low edge of the forest,
Mr and Mrs M. loading their small truck,
driving each other to the end in the dim air

and a bright rocket silver-yellow heavenwards,
airliner up in the last day there.

IX

North Kyoto

Rubbling up a bothy to pass off as me

An eddy, a tumour, bits
accreted round my life as merely irritant

which dispersed, things to go on as they were.

I leak frequently
it interrupts my nights

A small mountain hut
in which to fade
(with peculiar inscriptions
in charcoal).

Hagoromo

I

Under the thick sheet of water
ribbed, rushing
an eye of air

A scattering of thin silver cigarette foils
on the black ash, like paper to the touch now they've been
     burned.
On the heap of rice-straw mats; then the flood from the
     typhoon took them.
Dislodged from her room with the carpet and the loose dust
     under it
and the padlocks.

Thin sticks in soft skin

mossed up, and unsheathed;
bark hanging from the wet wood

in this dark bowl of the woods
where nothing changes
the sky silvered
with a stirring of the fronds against the light.

What was intended to be a root, of a tree,
and now the moss grows from it,
hanging in air.
And the other root, like a beard
with water-drops hanging from it
from the stream.

The road snakes round the hill
                and hugs it

Motif: the monotone
(steppes: Mali wastes)
where the plough turns
under the digue;
comes, and returns
unendingly.

Gleam, glisten, glide under the rock
where the old beard of fine roots drips;
pulse of a tiny wave over the moss

and now the bamboo-leaves will tremble
from the melting on them.

Little wormlets
at all angles over the bark
but not random;
flecks, nail-marks
on a silky dull green
in patterns.

Strange regularities
in the burrowings of the creatures
in the soft mud under the water
where I drink my drink for my
dead wife and wash my face.

Shaggy boiled crud, for bark
rhythms of ridge
open up,
ridges become cleft,
and re-fold

Silent wood
the woodpecker quietly
off,
and the crow echoing.

II

Light let in on the
wreckage of last year's snows

green, mottled, rotting.

A little stand of mushrooms
along the groin of a meadow
under bamboos;

two streams of mist
so slowly, quietly rising
from behind the mountain.

Brown lip
where the bloodied scar of the trunk
drools, scarf'd
and welded.

The Jardin du Luxembourg,
driving back on black coffee from Arles;
what rage, what hate, what misery.

A trickle sound in the forest
and the leaf falls

Watching the light grow
crook'd in the arm of this tree
while the crows all around
                              Aw, Aw,

III

Leaves, shadow-lapping

rust and thick yellow, with green

her clothes (her sweep?)
her colours

translucent brush-strokes for ribs
like an insect-pod Christ by Cimabue
but with more sense of what are muscles.

A crow straggles its way across the void
to meet them,
the fiery flood
across these uncompanionable peaks

where the bamboos
grind against each other
for the coming winter.

Burning firewood, for baths
smouldering rice-hulls, for ash

the tobi circles around and doesn't find much,
the mice having gone to ground;
so that one is grateful for the red berries that stand out
and the thin peppers that glow
and orange fires under plumes,
and for any sunset without clouds
that slows down the waning of the light a little longer.

The wild boar (or tanuki?) now shit ginkgos
with the nuts mostly intact
and a mush of digested flesh round them;
the old crow still hangs by the jaw
slicked down by the rain, over the weeks,
in the silence.

The hill of rice-husks
has a bunch of old bamboo stakes stuck in from the top
to let the air in as it burns.
The sharp odour.

Fierce orange-red
under couch-grass:
her colour,
my smell.

Small paddyfields
with rounded yellow-green grass banks bounding them in.

Coming down in sunlight through a broken glade
Thinking of my wife as she then was

'Good morning Mr Sheeps';
'Whoops!' for the tail of a rabbit, vanishing

Tensing and Silo in the snow;
in the Portobello Road, 6 a.m., baring her bum to a fire-hydrant.

The ink puckers the paper
at the knots where the brush turned,
pulling the strength in.

shoes, detective stories, matchboxes, her major remains
washed away as ash when the river rose

So that at last she put her all into it
(tout pour l'art)

Abandoned (when she went to London)
but not let go.

IV

The pale cream of the circle of the lower sun
through the drifting grey,
cloud off the mountain;

the streamer bunches up round the flaming wheel,
wreathes it in shroud,
hides it again.

The snow, a stole
hanging off the branch of this tree.

There is the lichen that lives under the stream, at full torrent. Flat
        to the rock, a dark dried-blood colour.
The long pocket of air, in the lee of a rock, that flips on and off
irregularly.

Strange convergence
this pattern, these flecks
on this hard wood, like limbs to the palm
that has the bark like loose socks
gunaikos, of woman, rucked up

gaunt bark, many-holed

round a vacancy.

Little scutterings of snow, trundling down the slope ahead,
diminishing.

The thick sough of the wind.

The soughing of a thousand trees, range to range, as the
        darkness closes.

V

but lo, the bracken sprouts
& curls
cet immense pouvoir
with the bronze-bright shaggy pelt
waiting to unfurl
spray of broken-down ferns
splayed from the centre
studded with them.

Colonies of pale and paler lichens
that meet like clouds or sea-wrack
and the bark already cracked

souls fade,
or there would be an encumbering in the world?
far-off surf in the pinetops
thick naked light on the scarred trunks

Leaf ironed out to a fullness,
old bamboo hard like ivory

a fullness; a stillness; present;
not etched but there.

always with their tops chawed off
tips chawed off
the great phalloi
bamboo thrusting out of the ground

the green not vivid but virulent
the flat mirror of water with the border of mud
with ragged banks
so flat, so delicate
waiting to be disturbed
with feet and with plantings.

and under the roughened,   fast-moving
water
the shadow of a frond, waving.

'I need *help!*'

huelp

Heavy surf, not far:
the storm working itself up in the treetops.
On the mountain, the cedars thrash,
the ribbed water rushing.

never bent
she knew she was a nuisance
never gave myself up to her
till 2–3 days before she died.

The halberds on the bronzes like these leaves;

the silvery-green fly-like creatures
flit about them intently.

VI

'You are very calm about all this'

horrent et tremunt
and into the drowning-boats

and out of the dark cabin, the voice of a radio
and the two lights of slightly different tones
the white and the slightly yellow

tussocks under snow.

Tired and glazed and as if pulled square by the plastic surgery
gazing at me
flatly, making no argument.

Betrayed and hiding nothing.

Keeping my options open:
ne manquez pas l'épisode où vous gagnez

> Under the thick sheet of water
> ribbed, rushing
> an eye of air.

A scattering of thin silver cigarette foils
on the black ash, like paper to the touch now they've been burned.

The first answer was always 'No'.

In the stillness
the watersound cut off by the pass
the wraiths move on the mountain
the tiny waterpattering
and the owl behind me.

A very remote light there down by the roadside
a bit like a firefly

the mountain blocked off by the mist
and then again the dog-barks.

Motif: the monotone,
with a little relief
and texturing,
senza struttura
architettura
gotta get above the field-line
to drink water without poison
to where the snow lies yet
unmelted

O ye whom
I pass by
when I pass by the Yodogawa Christian Hospital
will you be satisfied?

with your monument, when I have made it
quod non imber edax

Afraid; dried; paralysed;
denying her.

Steadily over the years

in small émiettements, witherings and closings:

> 'When I have got this done,
> then we will have castles in Spain.'

> con smalti, with tiles, with green and blue
> and the dark spaces in the garden
> where you will be

Bluffly accepting her, denying her.

Eat some more raisins,
couple the synapses,
gender more words.

VII

'Why did you take my bright cloak?

I will never get back to heaven-road now; wander
this keck-end of world
lonely for brightness;

Give me back my bright cloak?'

Flitting souls
wander in this waste,
not knowing what they have done,
that it was their chance;

that they blurred it, mucked it around
like a cat with a shrew, or a flower
kicked to death by passers-by;
and wonder why Dante was Dante. You
will have to wait
                    in the land of nothing
while your sister eats.

Neck of the Woods

I

The twig knuckle being caught
lifts up a curl of clear water;
ancient of days.

A small pulse, irregular,
down this groove

arising from the play of water-flow
      round the leaves and the brown cedar-spray
as they sway
caught under water.

After each pulse a strange slow dimple
across the pool.
Difference of temperature?

And then at last a movement up in the cleft
where the water also moves:
not the stream, but a living waterlouse.

II

Mandibles, proboscis
the ant and the loplop bug

a small stand of mushrooms
along the groin of a meadow
under bamboo.

Ferns about to burst out of the ground;
mayfly dancing above the waterflow;
every event in this stream is an irregular wave.

III

A huge wasted-out tree-stump
almost alevel with the ground
with the firm young upstanding fern-shoots
higher than it,
some bowed,
some curled up,
ready to rise. And now I've trud on one;
no longer ready to rise.

That wrinkle in the water
that stays,
that fold in the glassy substance
where the fold meets another fold
and is itself ribbed:

1. Silver drop
at about-one-second intervals
down a dark frond

2. Every third pulse, or so
the wave over the rock dwindles
and the ribs start to dry

3. The bird overhead, per-
petually
an unsatisfied scale of five notes.

Waves and wrinkles,
back-wrinkling across the pond,
meet and disperse.

IV

In the vast cavernous hole
millions of work-hands
on ladders, with buckets,
rising and falling
in a centipede-like movement,
like the wind passing over fronds
or the flow of a centipede's legs
rising unendingly.

V

St John's pulpit
now gone, now rotted:
an old sock, dimpled with orange
and bent over like a limp finger
beckoning.

In the stream, under a tomb of living lead
the little bug has implanted itself
very firmly in the side of the living rock.
The twig has stopped rocking,
somehow locked;
only the thickening water over it, in waves,
makes it seem to move.

A dollop of snow lands on the rock,
diverting the pulse;
the pulse melts it;
but for a while it was changed,
changing some other rhythm
downstream.

VI

Wail, and cry from the unknown creature on my left
to the unknown creature on my right.

The open maw full of fungus.

Little gleam of sun on the lower part of a tree-trunk;
this was a meadow.

Tree rockets off to the left
to start a new life.

Here a deer lay.

Little fists of fern-ends,
grass growing out of a crack in an old stump.

And the bubble with the rhythm of a heartbeat
and the dangling hairs as if from a twat
with the beads of water on them
evermore thrown up by the stream.

VII

The leaf-edge lifts
and lifts
on the water,
but not regularly;
the whole mass of them, leaves and cedar-fronds, shakes
        like a belly,
irregularly,
and on the upturned leaves
the globes of water wobble, but don't move.

Percepticules

Pause at the same spot
and break off a knuckle from the
same dead bamboo to pick my teeth with.

frog
in the endless recesses of the moss
the rock as if speaking

Oily slate-grey
boar-turds renewed after
some weeks' absence.

The tiny rain-drops floating
like small insects in the air,
the bamboo glitters

silent triangular grin
distended with a mouse
of whom visible: the tail

Antennae out for the word-drift,
the wrinkling in the surface of the water.

Walled up with my books,
the almost-inaudible child's voice
and the white sky

Scrambled rapidly up its
invisible rope and paused
about one inch from the ceiling.

tiny spider
scuttering over a well-polished deer-pellet

Air heavy with chrysanthemums
in Nara, and old Buddhas.

with its naked-Makin head,
nudging about along the edge of the leaf,
leaving the tiny green grasshopper be

the tanuki puts its turds
smack at each end of the riverbridge,
smack in the middle.

The cloud of birds
resolves out to a line on a wire,
falls off into a cloud again.

The cedars heave in the wind
like old counsellors,
each with his woe.

The almost-silent song
of the toilet-cleaner,
dreaming of her sons and of her youth.

Honoured to be another worn pole
in the autumn air
for the dragonflies to sit on.

Gaunt branches beyond
and on each branch
a crow.

Rippleshadow down the line of spiderweb,
segments of light

Dragonfly borne on an upbreeze
past the soft bamboo
waving.

And I also, were I a deer,
on the broad back of a promontory
so I could see them a long time coming.

The trees are denuding themselves
the better to receive
the shock of winter.

A crow on a light-pole
bodes. Voices,
and a tennis-ball

Bite into a persimmon
and the great bell sounds,
Hou ryuu ji

A million huge spiders
probing the ground towards each other tentatively
(tussocks under snow)

Deer crossing the ridge in mist
with a stiff silent
bound.

green plant slowly liberates
itself from under snow as the sun warms.

Pale land-crab of spring,
the cautious ballet of the six feet.

*The Nara poem is from Basho (1644–1694); the Hyouruuji,
from Shiki (1866–1902).*

Shore-wrack

The edges of the erosion-marks showing up very clear
because the sun has just come out from the rain-clouds,

                                  early autumn 8 a.m.,
with the cry of the single deer repeated and quiet and tentative.
The multiple fungi stacked in ranks up the tree-side
no longer quite white, because they have mould on them.

Stacked up in ranks on the tree-side
no longer white,
having light mould on them. No

longer quite
light, have a white
mould on them.

Moss never grows on bamboo.

Moss grows like bull's cullions
off the edge of these roots,
a virid green
in the dark.

A snake like a wet branch, with no bark.

These things are as they are, I didn't make them;

I can arrange them;

or
    part of me can,
the part with bull's cullions and strange bark.

Come to me, poem, like a deer-shriek
in the dark.

On seeing the multiple-array deep-space telescopes in the
Atacama Desert, Chile, brought to bear

He himself is a bead, some 3 mm. across;
the rest very long legs.
He moves zigzaggedly
on the fragments of leaves
and twigs: at every step,
two or three of his legs flinchingly

touching out his way.

One foot away from my yellow boot,
he has no idea that I'm there.
I move my boot,
                    he flees,
his scheme of the cosmos
redrawn.

Up there in the sun, in the green
cedar tops,
where the light laps,

is the real surface of the earth

for the birds,

but not for me,
down here among the murky trunks
and deer-tracks.

And the mole thinks:
up there
among the deer-tracks and trunks

is the real surface of the earth;

but not for me, down here
among the roots
and air-gaps.

    There, you
walk free.

knows that he is the secret of
the universe but won't say and is
pretending to be a caterpillar.
He is trying to contemplate his navel,
but his muscles being out of condition
won't reach that far; when he
attains to that beatific position, then
you may look up and see the
stars go out,

        one by one,
for the circle will have closed,
thou wilt be
That,

    Ah,
Oh.

    Go,
therefore,
and be at peace with one another
meanwhile.

On seeing an old warhorse brought out to work again in 2001

B52s waiting to bomb them into democracy, still the best
       weapon we have for some jobs,
can be over target anywhere in Afghanistan
within 15 minutes; within seconds target is in pieces,
under walls, in fragments, usually hard to identify;
still the best weapon we have for some jobs;

bring with them a whole history, forty years back,
of making mush carpet out of villages:
rice fields: water buffalo; pieces of burned target;
target doesn't know anything about that,
but is probably beginning to understand about democracy.

Abbaye Saint-Victor, Marseille

A piece was splitting away between the cut vertical of a letter and the surface to the right; the experienced eye could see it; nothing to be done; a touch would detach it.

After some 1,900 years commemorating the deaths of two brothers, *sub vi maris*: 'under the power of the sea.' Deaths caused no doubt by a failure of rigging, keel, or some other point where the *vis maris* would have been too much for it: as the skilled eye might have foreseen.

The lightening (loss of transparency) of the stone; the fine canting of the surface relative to the stone surrounding it: the eye can know. The names of the brothers no longer definite; which god their mother was invoking no longer clear: possibly Christ, possibly Serapis; not enough letters left to show that, now.

A very slight raining of powder from the damp mortar in this part of the sub-basement of the church: aged, probably, only about 900 years.

Pulled from my vocabulary of sounds
a bunch of
thin strips of plywood
that had been out too long
in the weather, peeling
off in layers,
very dry, being
rattled in air.

Looked up and saw it was
two pigeons taking off towards the river.

not different in colour,
nor in shape,
or size, particularly,
from the streaks
of moss under the water pulsing over the rock
below the fall; but

as the glass slides over the fall, and the sheets fold
and are thrown into turbulence,
and the whole rock shifts, to the eye,
with the water that wells over it,

one small fleck under the pulse
creeps, hesitates,
and moves back again

The ant-lion is an insect. He constructs a pit about one inch across, with sides of loose sand. He waits at the bottom, hidden; when an ant blunders into his pit it cannot get out, and he dines. Occasionally you may see him at work, perfecting his pit, hurling out unwanted items with vigorous flicks.

A niche in the rock, by the steep path below the dam
up to the woods:
someone has built a smooth ledge for a shrine,
and now in the dust I see three coins, for the gods who
bless the wayfarers passing this way.

The dust, whether from frost shifting the rocks
or from insect-works,
falls slowly on the ledge and builds up; in it
seven ant-lions have made their neat inns, to welcome
wayfarers the gods let stray.

Leaf tumbling across the cold space between here and the far
    mountain,
tufts of smoke from the early bath blown between here and the
    tree.
Hands crackle like parchment stretched across bone, when I
    stretch them;
soon the light fades, soon I shall be driven out
from my empty eyrie to see the last sun on the hills
before it all dims down to the shadows creeping below.
Bright triangle of trees stripped bare on the hill, where the deer
    find the sun's warmth
and have it stripped from them by the wind;
persimmons sit on their twigs here in their own calm air
waiting for winter to blacken them if birds don't come.
Maybe a bear, that black square high up in the triangle of bare
    trees?
Too still: it would freeze in the gusts that blow about the
    bamboo on the hillside below.
No drama, no companion, no antagonist to remove
the flatness and emptiness and whatness of what is
in a long winter valley on the back side of Japan on an empty
    afternoon.

don my prophylactic,
my bear-bell,
and plunge into the dark wood.

There is that under these snow-drifts
which will be a toad

                      when the time comes,
giving voice to the mosses

and because the split is there
where the water took the rock, say
forty years back, along a fault laid down by this lava
perhaps four billion
years ago,
so that the splayed-out
stream, or part of it, over the stone above,

                                     flows like glass

to where the split lets
half fall away and rush down,
and half
ride over the rock,

till it meets the edge and drops down
to meet the rest,

there is this fine crook-back
wavering
in the lower stream,
which is no more than
the line where the one flow meets the other, and is whipped
       away again:
meeting,
making this line,
borne away again

The calm breast of the mountain
is made of
cedars snow-dusted

Tree, twisting around
for a hold in the rocks,
but the stream works

Just basking;
resting;
turning the bits of housefly he's just eaten
into the shadow of transparent
red wings
on white wall

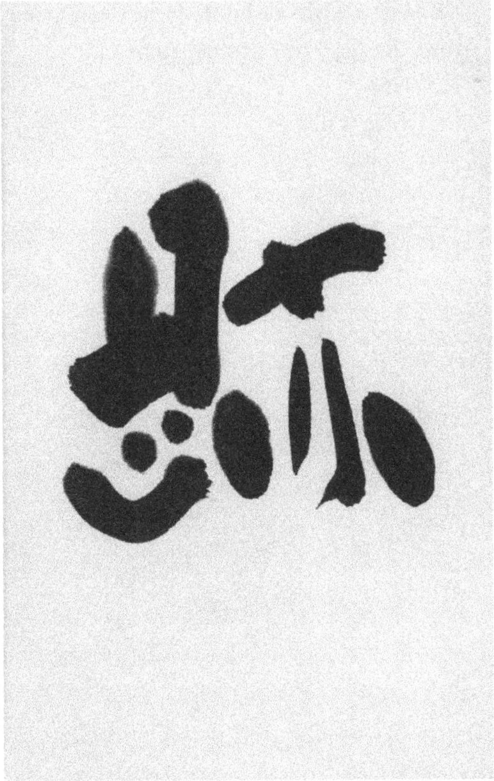
跡

Ato

跡   mark; print; trace; track

Stella Irene Correa obit 15.12.97

from the snare of the hunters, and from the sharp word
(de laqueo venantium, et de verbo aspero)

thou shalt not be afraid of the terror of the night
of the arrow that flieth in the day, of the business that
                                   walketh about in the dark
of invasion, or of the noonday devil.

In their hands they shall bear thee up:
lest thou dash thy foot against a stone

thou shalt walk upon the asp and the basilisk;
leonem et draconem conculcabis.

I will protect her, because she hath known My name.

O so sweet, o so gentle
light,

and these banks;

suddenly adown the angle
a crow's shadow, and more slowly
across the path;

and I look again, and see the stump
way up on the scoop of hill
from which I looked down on this path
where she walked, then in snow,

now in this light,
with the crow's shadow.

Slithering down snow, grabbing branches that
shower me with snow while I try to
stop and fix images relating to pattern
for the book of patterns we would have
writ: comes to mind that photograph
of her, descending a slope in snow in
large boots with her cats, the thick
fur jacket, the high collar, the solid her
and her smile, before ever
we began. The bamboos
wait to crack / under the snow.

If I cleared this room so I could
sleep in it,   or contemplate in it,

the days would be dull, or summer come
and be intolerably humid
so I will sit here

surrounded by clutter

'From Correa's Room
To Be Sorted'
suitcases
clothes hanging along the verandah
blocking the view

and the litter of her intentions
and my intentions, now that I no longer
think it worth while to intend

not quite in sight of the sprays of white
orchids outside the back-room window;

and drink in the quiet, and the rubbed pillar,
and the broken plaster dropping flakes of
dried mud, the smooth tatami
and the sound of the bee passing
towards the quince flowering
and the quiet;

Tiny circle on my
forearm, rainbow-colours, concentric,
4 mm. across, seen through my eye half-
closed, sleeping on the grass in front of
the Natural History Museum.

Lie / sun / bake /
warm through / drift down, open eye
to groups of tourists on the lawn.

Arm all criss-crossed, light hairs, / one of these
refracting, apparently, bright glimmering circle
of circles, rippled, spectrum-colours,
4 mm. across, gleaming at me.

Every time my heart beats, all the colours shift
back, and across again. Whump;
whump.

The *châsses* from
Limoges in the V&A: in the sea of blue the small
flowers of circles, green, red, sliced
through, small worlds,
flowering of creation in the blue.

Light from the sun: X million miles.
Hair on my arm, splitting
the light, to my eye, the target: only
this one circle of rainbows, rippled:

no other hair on my arm makes this light.

A small black dot on the grass,
insect, moving towards my eye; blow it away. And now
impossible to find the spectrum again.

And you do not even know
whether she would have liked it:
your broad bands, in blue
and the other colours you do not even know
the names of;

azurite, malachite
splotched blue

Working over the husks
now my wife's gone.

Bamboo

Pour n'aboutir à rien;
but still fixed like a rock

innumerable beard of small roots,
capillaries ranked
the finer ones near the outside / like pinheads
now feeding nothing:

on a cru bon d'en finir
with a diagonal slice

Because I only have this porridge of
sifted-down words, / left-overs from
studying, with which to hint at

guessed-at
networks

Downwind of the light,
the streamers of photons leave my pee-
                    stream its
shadow, flagging the thin column.
The steam rises.

with the fields
hunkering down for winter, with their sides
mowed of sedge, banking up from the valley
and nobody moving on them now;

I will take this path
below where I sat six years gone
in the cold breeze reading Dante and
wondering whether one could live in this valley and still live.

Gleam of moon, behind clouds,
the thin slice, bright sickle
seen from Coventry when she was afar off
in Canada / 25 years gone

Kabe after work and the
huge hill out of the valley in the dusk,
stepping out from school, and you from your riverbank;
23 years?

The layers on layers, like the hills that go back blue
                                        on blue-grey
over what one knows to be banal one-supermarket valleys
below them in the folds, invisible
under their march into who knows what beyond.

Into the drear, the old
rice fields now under the cedars,

even the cedars neglected and the wisteria has its
                    bite-marks deep into this one.

Trickle of water feeding nothing but the mulch the deer
                    step in and even the moss finds it hard to
                    live in this.

Into the dark where the millions of work-hands laboured
                    in the light to build
rice-walls now darkened over with pines
and the deer-steps now drag the sand down to undifferentiatedness

This was a path; this was a terrace;
it was a good path,
broad, and with a steady climb

little, limpid, translucent
pale yellow-green umbrella of leaves on the paper-tree

and the slab of verdigris rock, with the fine angle
I bring you these

?treasures

the tremor
of the drop, in the light
and the stretched-out twigs
finding space

how happy I am to come out to sun / on segmented rock
mushroom-cups march up the trunk,
orange edges to light

some bug has planted its bole in this leaf

'It's only physical'

I would say, when I told her I loved her

All over and down the combe the water drove the black
          stones, roaring
in the night of the typhoon while it dumped its rain;
now only the silent sun and the tussocks gleaming
and the gaunt trunk and the trickle of the stream
in the day again.

Alley of mourners;
half a grove gone in the night
and the gentle snow still coming.

*The snowfall is heavy but the temperatures not cold; often the
snow falls and clings to the bamboo and builds up until the
bamboo bows over to the ground. From time to time in the
silence you will hear the crack, like a rifle-shot, of one breaking.*

Philosophical letter to his father

Dear Noël

      The stars in their courses follow ruts like
wrinkles in the sky, which we can't see but the
Lord sees when he holds out a certain light to
illuminate them by, thinking: Them pore mortals
think stars run free, like bowls on a lawn, but I know
when I holds up the cosmos like
a caul with its skein
            the stars don't run free, they
    follow my wrinkles.

So.

Ghosts of that grove groping up
to the dead moon; skeins of old wisteria holding down
these trees; I am a shadow, through which blows
mainly, you.

Standing alone amid the wild waste
jotting down your notes
and yet you always think there'll be someone there
to read what you're saying

standing alone in the wild waste
making your notes.

The steel blue light down in the holes of the snow.

Wisteria welted by its own tendons
        on its way to strangling a cherry;
                                        long gone,
and the only part not rotted is the part where the wisteria's tendril
holds the shiny-bronze bark in its gripe.

Silence.
Running water; wind, and the sun,
and again silence.
At strange angles; the wisteria's weight
ought to have pulled the tree down by now,
but it still holds, though the ghostly rot is through
        to the quick   the vermiculation

Tonight my star a little clouded;
moon in mist;
she will remember these terraces,
rich and black,
with red flowers.

the vertical cloud holding the mountain
drifts, and the mountain clears,
and the small edge with the trees
                  in the gap
is now the long back of the mountain.

And the ridges boil off their mists;
now shrouded again.

At my feet
the lichen moulded over the rock-edge,
the leaves rot down with spring.

So slim
the forearm, the wrist
of the deer lying in the forest
path

bone white,
but with still enough gristle to articulate.

No sign of the deer.

On the ridge the green translucent
leaves
and the silence and bird-cries;
down the side the dark army
in blotches of light.

The path up by the stream,
stuffing the holes with spores
while Mr Mori, stalwart
thwocked the hard wood;

for a few days' delight, blighted
by my indifference

To grow mushrooms, logs of a hard wood called kunugi *have to be cut and stacked in long rows under the cedars, to be punched with holes for the spores, with a sort of sledge-hammer.*

There is a little low beat
lower than a woodpecker,
                    which I thought it might be.

It is the train to Kinosaki, and what we didn't do there.

Falls into the forms of his anger

rage and vindication and anger

Voices of the children drift and fade
late sun on the feet on the desk in a silent room
remembering.

Till this bitter hole becomes another memory
or frame into which to pour buckets of wanhope
though it itself was just a place in which I
sat and remembered.

Your heaven

Beauteous light, with greens and blues
with leaves overlapping
in a forest torn by strange winds

and there lurks Junior Junior
hiding her children

Stop, clap hands to *hotoke*
or rather 3 grey graves huddled by corner field

Crow leaves contrail of shite, looping
                                        down thru air;

Mountain broods,
hiding sun gone down through earth to
                                        come back up again.

Dipper homing squawks
its small squawk through dim air

whither, O world shall I grasp hold of you
precisely no further on than I was
            yesterday though she was with me

And then to remember it at sundown
when the light falls from the village
and the world is full of things that
                                    never were
but only in my mind
when you come to me in my dreams and
                    make me jealous again

All around the glowering green
valley sinking into dusk
and the leaping orange   (fire)

Daily with what the sun leaves
(pink rag over the hill)
rice heads growing stronger

Translucent leaves imprinted on
leaves, so you can't tell which is leaf
and which shadow; glowing green.
Shrieking starling, across the void;
silent hawk; returns.
Clouds marching steadily.

There is only the void, which is filled with
these things temporarily. There was the yellow
sun in the long grass outside Collow.
My mind passes / the dead holes at the
roots of trees up this slope. Limbs of
trees hanging in living trees, out of
Carpaccio. The hawk cries.

Outside the garden, in the wheelchair on the gravel
'si me amas, paullum hic ades'
but I would not

The lead sky, the dead fruit-tree
straggling
        over the gravel, small pieces of grey

In here is all sunlight, and I look up at
these leaves, in this forest
come to me love
          if you love me, paullum hic ades

Pines;
and the wind soughs;
and my wife says,
What are you doing?
and I don't know

Everywhere, remotely,
the wind-sough;

the clear plop
of the nightingale.

Noon sighs:
c'est vite fait.
soon done

Light, from the layering rice-fields
down to the stream;
from the sky;
                fades;

2 lamps
in the thick
dark,
                and the deer-shriek.

Now only a dog-bark
and the passing car,
and the mountain
heavy with night.

The clouds, ever rising,
ever reaching up
never reaching
over me;

only the light
left pale in the patches of the sky
and the deer-shriek.

Burning sickle just cutting
the mountain-top
hidden in cloud.

Lightning Source UK Ltd.
Milton Keynes UK
UKHW01f0643111018
330371UK00001B/186/P